MY BODY™

My Lungs

Kathy Furgang

The Rosen Publishing Group's
PowerKids Press™
New York

For Michael

Published in 2001 by The Rosen Publishing Group, Inc.
29 East 21st Street, New York, NY 10010

First Edition

Book Design: Kim Sonsky

Illustration Credits: All organ 3-D illustrations © LifeArt/TechPool Studios, Inc.; All other 3-D illustrations by Kim Sonsky.
Photo Credits: Pp. 5, 16, 19 © Photo Researchers.

Furgang, Kathy.
  My lungs / by Kathy Furgang.
    p. cm. — (My body)
  Includes index.
  Summary: Describes the parts of the lungs and respiratory system, how they function, and problems that can affect them.
  ISBN 0-8239-5575-3 (lib. bdg. : alk. paper)
  1. Lungs—Juvenile literature. 2. Respiration—Juvenile literature. [1. Lungs. 2. Respiration.] I. Title.

QP121 .F87 2000
612.2—dc21   99-088033

Manufactured in the United States of America

Contents

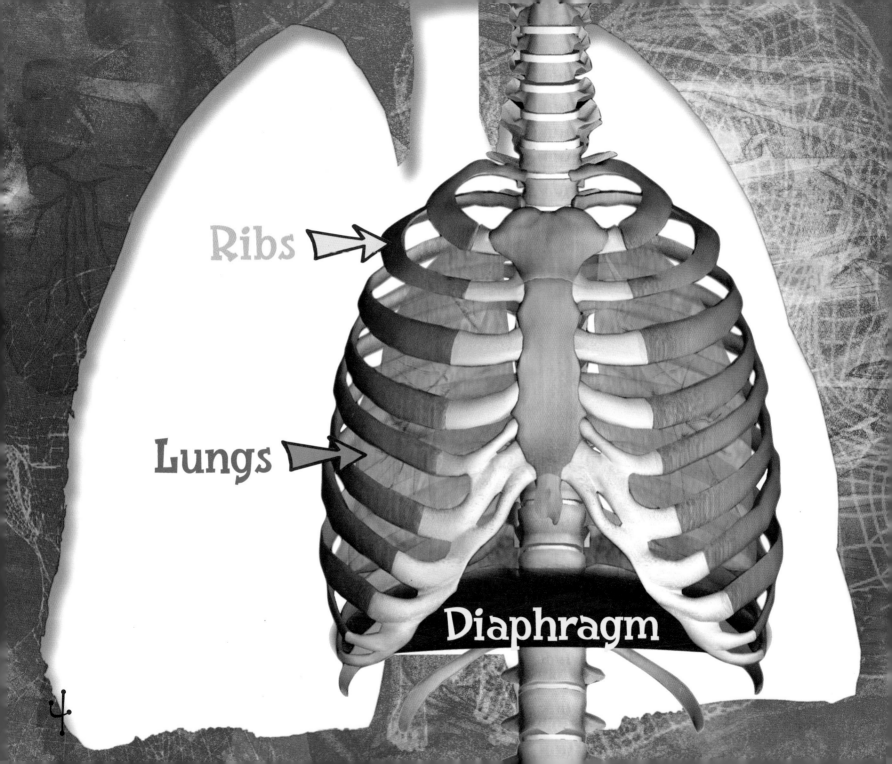

Ribs

Lungs

Diaphragm

Your Breathing Body

Every time you breathe in and out, your lungs are hard at work. You have two lungs, and you need them to breathe and stay alive. They are found inside your chest. Ribs are the bones in your chest that surround your lungs and keep them safe. Your lungs start at the top of your ribs. Your ribs are just below your neck. The bottoms of your lungs reach a thin, curved muscle called your **diaphragm**. Your diaphragm separates your chest from your stomach. It helps you when you breathe.

Your left and right lungs are spongelike. In a CAT scan (on this page), an image is made by computerized tomography. This means that X rays are used to take a picture of the lungs.

A Breathing Machine

When you breathe in air, it enters your body through your nose or your mouth. On the way to your lungs, air passes your **voice box**. It then enters a large pipe called the **trachea**. Your trachea, which is also called your windpipe, travels down your chest. This pipe then branches off into two smaller tubes called **bronchi**. Each bronchial tube brings air to one of your lungs. Once air is in your lungs, the air goes to different tubes that get smaller. At the ends of these tubes are tiny air sacs called **alveoli**. You have about 300 million alveoli in each lung! When you breathe out, the air travels back on the same route and passes your voice box again. The movement of the air across your voice box helps you speak.

The alveoli are tiny round air sacs that look like grapes attached to the ends of tiny branches.

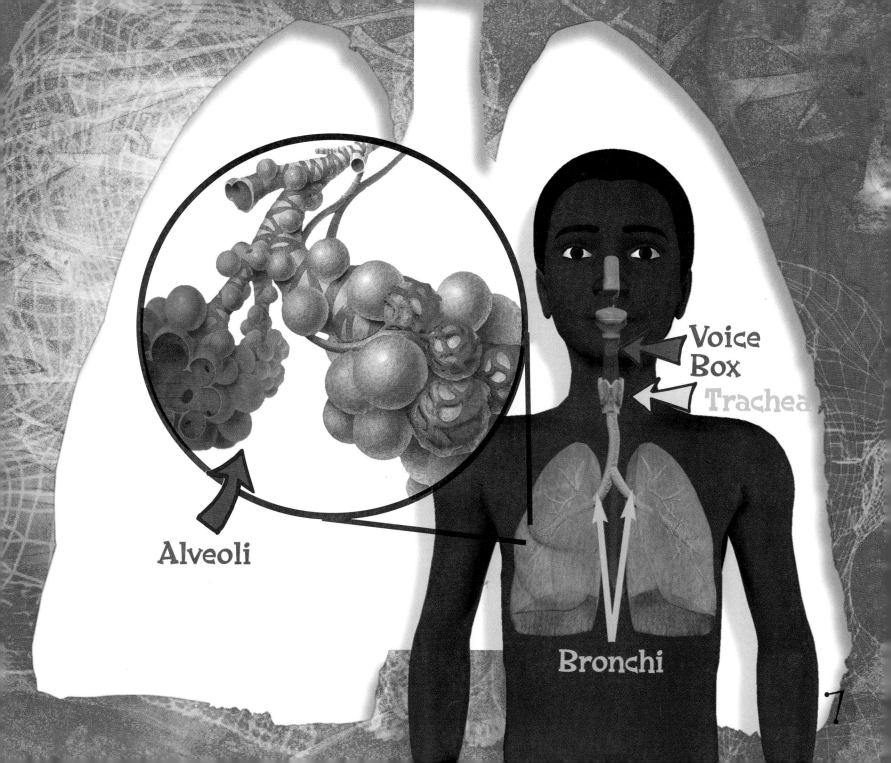

Alveoli

Voice
Box

Trachea

Bronchi

7

How Do You Breathe?

Take a deep breath. Did you see your chest move out? Each time you breathe, you get some help from your ribs and diaphragm. When you breathe in air, or inhale, your diaphragm tightens and straightens out. Your ribs push up and out when you inhale. Your chest looks as if it's getting bigger as your lungs fill up with air. Your lungs stretch out just like a balloon. When you exhale, or breathe out, your diaphragm loosens up. Your lungs push the air out and get smaller.

When you blow up a balloon, you inhale first. Your diaphragm tightens, straightens, and then pushes out your ribs. When you exhale to blow air into the balloon, your diaphragm relaxes and your ribs move inward.

Good Air In, Bad Air Out

There is a gas in the air that your body needs to stay alive. This gas is called **oxygen**. When you breathe in, oxygen enters your lungs. It is then carried throughout your body by your blood. All parts of your body need oxygen to work correctly. Your body uses oxygen to burn food for energy. When this happens, a gas called **carbon dioxide** is made. Carbon dioxide is a waste. A waste is something that your body cannot use. The carbon dioxide is carried through your blood and back to your lungs. Your lungs push the carbon dioxide back out into the air to get rid of it. This process is called respiration.

When you inhale, you breathe in oxygen. When you exhale, you breathe out carbon dioxide. The act of breathing in and out is called respiration.

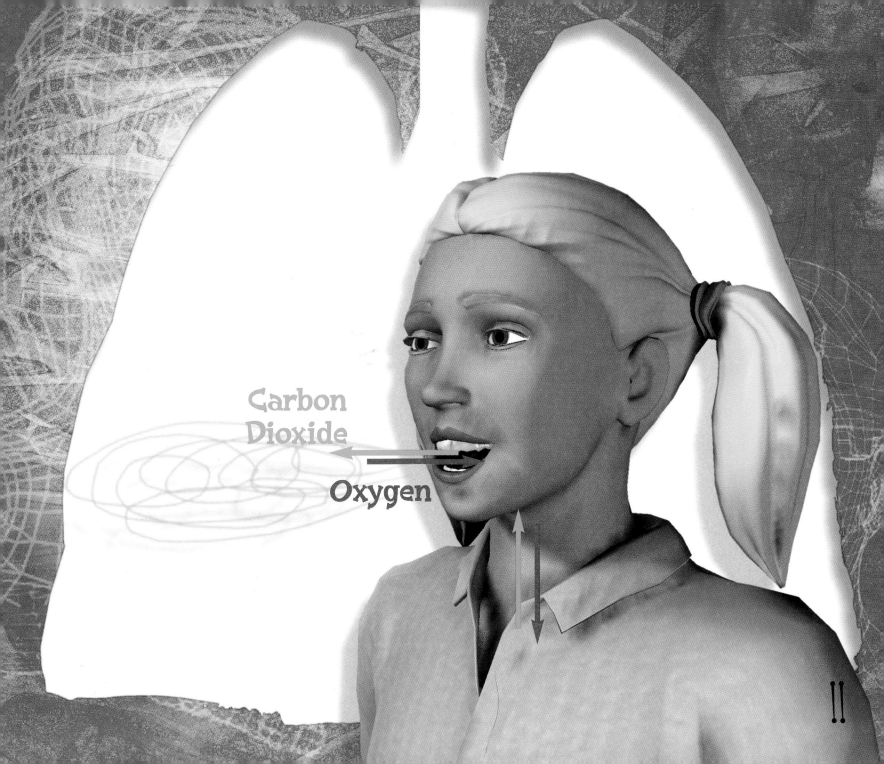

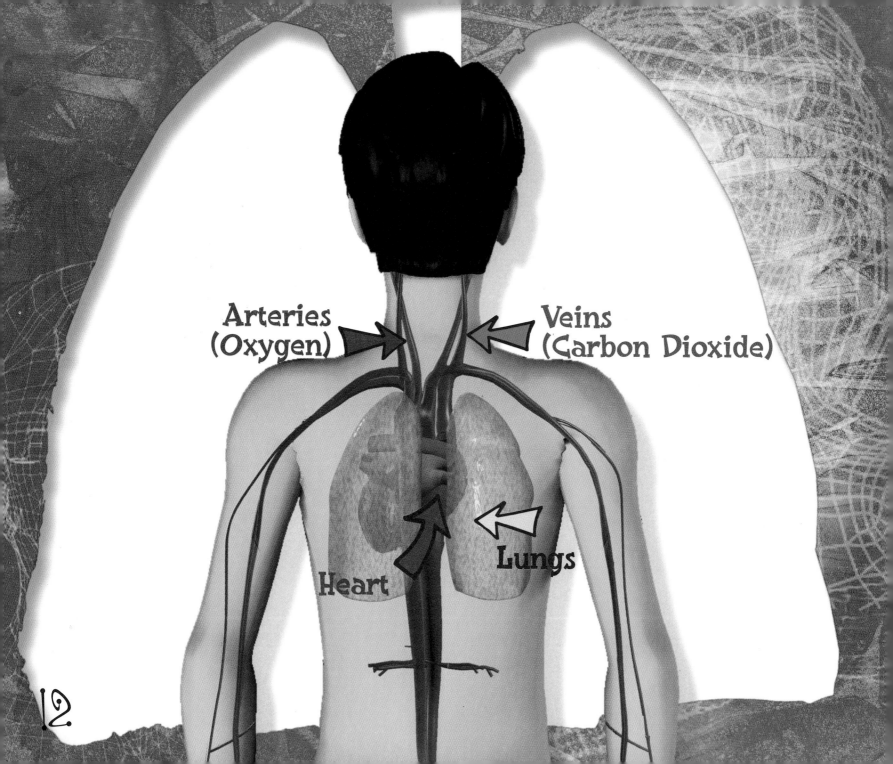

Arteries
(Oxygen)

Veins
(Carbon Dioxide)

Heart

Lungs

12.

Help From Your Heart

Oxygen and carbon dioxide do not go in and out of just your lungs. Your heart pumps these gases all around your body through your blood. Your heart delivers the blood to the rest of your body through tubes called arteries. When blood is low in oxygen and has a lot of carbon dioxide, it travels back to your heart through tubes called veins. Your heart pumps it back to your lungs. Then your lungs remove the carbon dioxide from the blood and replace it with rich oxygen. Fresh blood gets sent back to your heart. Then it is pumped through your body. The system of your heart and its blood vessels, such as arteries and veins, that moves blood throughout your body is called your **circulatory system**.

Every beat of your heart means that more blood is being sent to and from your lungs. Your circulatory system moves blood throughout your body.

Making Mucus

Your body has special ways to keep itself from becoming sick. Your trachea is lined with a thick, sticky matter called **mucus**. Mucus keeps dirt and germs from reaching your lungs. Tiny hairs inside your trachea push the germ-filled mucus up into your throat or nose. These hairs are called **cilia**. You can then get rid of the mucus by coughing, clearing your throat, or blowing your nose. When you get sick, your body makes more mucus so it can fight off the illness.

If germs get all the way into your lungs, special cells there can attack and kill them. It is better, though, if your body can fight and kill the germs before they reach your lungs.

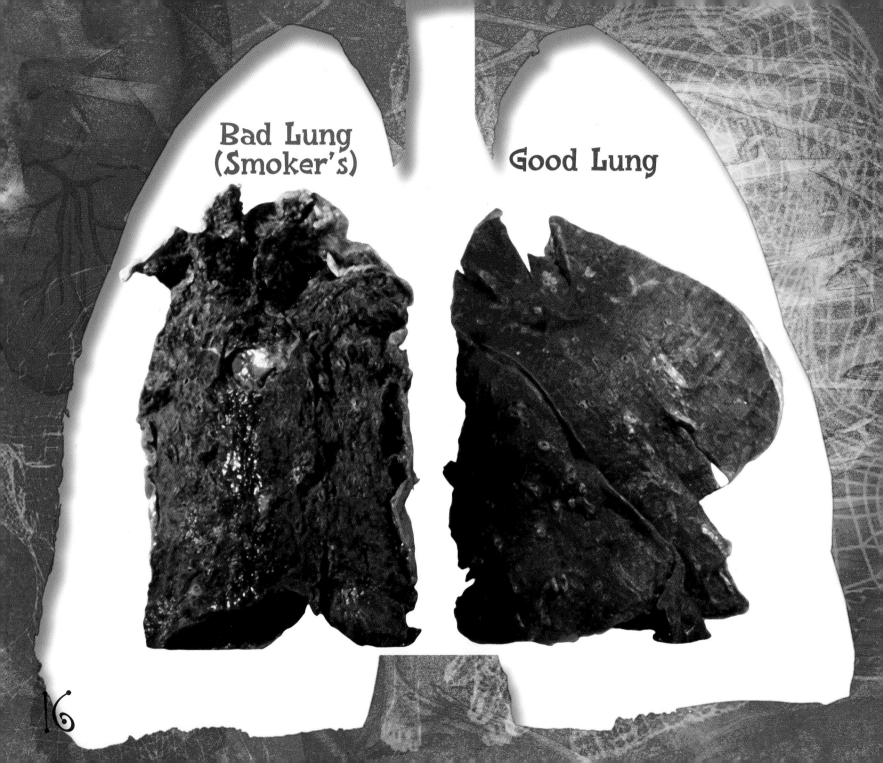

Dirty Lungs

Sometimes dirt gets through to your lungs and causes harm. The natural color of your lungs is pink. When you breathe in dirt and smoke, however, your lungs become gray and dark. City air has more dirt and pollution than country air. Sometimes this dirt and pollution can harm the lungs. Some people hurt their lungs by smoking. Breathing in smoke from cigarettes is very bad for your lungs. Cigarette smoke makes it hard for you to breathe and turns your lungs black. Many of the people who die from a serious disease called **lung cancer** are smokers.

These pictures show a smoker's bad lung and another person's good lung. Smoking causes harm to the cilia in your trachea. The cilia are meant to stop dirt and germs from entering your lungs.

Lung Diseases

Your right lung has three parts, or **lobes**. Your left lung has two lobes. Sometimes people can live without one of the lobes if it is damaged from a disease. When people have problems with their lungs, they often cough and have trouble breathing. One way that doctors can tell what is wrong is by taking an **X ray**. An X ray is a special picture that can show what the inside of a person's body looks like. Lung cancer is a disease that causes a harmful growth on the lungs. The growth looks like a shadow on the X ray. **Bronchitis** is another sickness that affects the lungs. Bronchitis is an infection of the bronchi, the tubes that bring air to the lungs. This infection can be treated with medicine.

The X ray at the top show the healthy lungs of a child. By using X rays, doctors can tell how healthy your lungs are. There are three lobes in your right lung and only two lobes in your left lung.

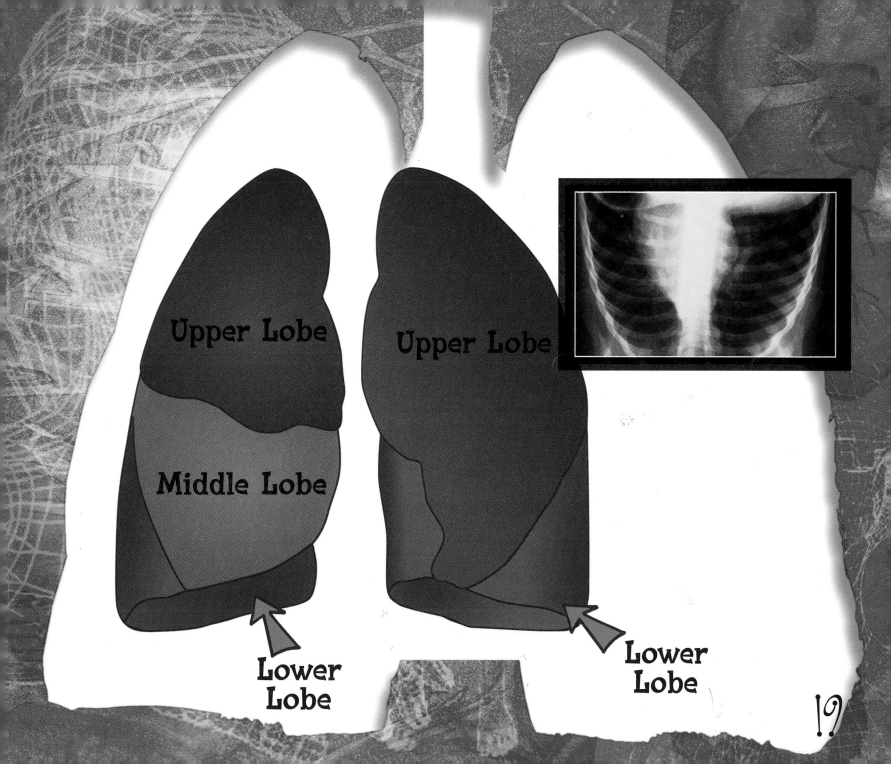

Upper Lobe

Upper Lobe

Middle Lobe

Lower
Lobe

Lower
Lobe

19

Other Lung Problems

Asthma is an illness in which the insides of the bronchi become narrower and make it difficult for a person to breathe. Many things, such as smoke, drugs, and even a cold, can trigger an asthma attack. There is no cure for asthma, but attacks can be prevented by avoiding the things that set them off.

Another lung problem is the lung disease called lung cancer. In the early 1960s, doctors found out how to do an operation for people who were dying of lung cancer. The operation is called a lung transplant. During a transplant, the patient's lung is taken out. A healthy lung from someone who has just died is put in its place. The outlook for people who have received transplants is improving.

Asthma attacks can be prevented by avoiding things that trigger them, such as cigarette smoke, pets, drugs, and dust. Asthma can be helped by using an inhaler, a tool that contains a spray with special medicine.

Keeping Healthy

The best way to keep your lungs healthy your whole life is to exercise and not smoke. When you exercise, your muscles work hard. They need extra energy and oxygen from your lungs. To deliver the extra oxygen your body needs during exercise, you breathe faster to bring more air into your lungs. This keeps both your heart and lungs healthy. The best exercises for your heart and lungs are running, swimming, bike riding, and any other activity that keeps your body moving.

Glossary

alveoli (ahl-VEE-oh-lee) Tiny sacs in the lungs that take in and send out air.

bronchi (BROHN-kee) Two tubes in the chest that bring air to each of the lungs.

bronchitis (brohn-KYH-tis) A sickness that involves the lungs and breathing.

carbon dioxide (KAR-bin dy-OK-syd) A gas that the body makes and then breathes out as waste.

cilia (SIH-lee-ah) Tiny hairs in different parts of the body that help to keep dirt from reaching the lungs.

circulatory system (SIR-kew-lah-tor-ee SIS-tehm) The path that blood travels through the body.

diaphragm (DYH-ah-frahm) The muscle below the lungs that helps in breathing.

lobes (LOWBZ) Parts of each lung.

lung cancer (LUNG KAN-suhr) A harmful growth on the lung that the body cannot fight off on its own.

lung transplant (LUNG TRANZ-plant) An operation that replaces an old lung in a very sick person with a healthy lung.

mucus (mew-KUS) Thick, sticky liquid in the body that helps to fight sickness.

oxygen (AHK-sih-jin) A gas in the air that has no color, taste, or odor, and is necessary for people and animals to breathe.

trachea (TRAY-kee-ah) The pipe that brings air down toward the lungs.

voice box (VOYS BOX) The body part that uses air to make sound and speech.

X ray (EKS RAHY) A special picture that can be taken of the inside of the body.

23

Index

A
air, 6, 9, 10, 17, 18, 22
alveoli, 6
arteries, 13
asthma, 21

B
bronchi, 6, 18, 21

C
carbon dioxide, 10, 13
cilia, 14
circulatory system, 13

D
diaphragm, 5, 9

H
heart, 13, 22

M
mucus, 14

O
oxygen, 10, 13, 22

R
respiration, 10
ribs, 5, 9

S
smoking, 17, 22

T
trachea, 6, 14

V
veins, 13
voice box, 6

W
waste, 10

Web Sites

To learn more about the lungs, check out these Web sites:

http://www.lung.ca/children/

http://www.imcpl.lib.in.us/nov_resp.htm

http://tqjunior.thinkquest.org/5785/

24